CODE

The Hunt

Tony Bradman ● **Jon Stuart**

Contents

OXFORD
UNIVERSITY PRESS

Macro Marvel
(billionaire inventor)

Welcome to Micro World!

Macro Marvel invented Micro World – a micro-sized theme park where you have to shrink to get in.

A computer called **CODE** controls Micro World and all the robots inside – MITEs and BITEs.

A MITE

A BITE

Disaster strikes!

CODE goes wrong on opening day.
CODE wants to shrink the world.

Macro Marvel is trapped inside the park …

Enter Team X!

Four micro agents – *Max, Cat, Ant* and *Tiger* – are sent to rescue Macro Marvel and defeat CODE.

Mini Marvel joins Team X.

Mini Marvel
(Macro's daughter)

In the last book ...

- Tiger battled a dragon.
- Cat distracted the dragon in her Bee-machine. Tiger escaped.
- The Dragon-BITE appeared!

**CODE key
(2 collected)**

You are in the Dragon Quest zone.

3

Before you read

Sound checker
Say the sound.

y

Sound spotter
Blend the sounds.

b	o	d	y

v	e	r	y

a	ng	r	y

n	ee	d

Tricky words
have
so

Into the zone

How can Mini find out about
the Dragon-BITE?

4

The Dragon-BITE

Mini got her Gizmo.
"I have to look up the
Dragon-BITE," she said.

Dragon-BITE

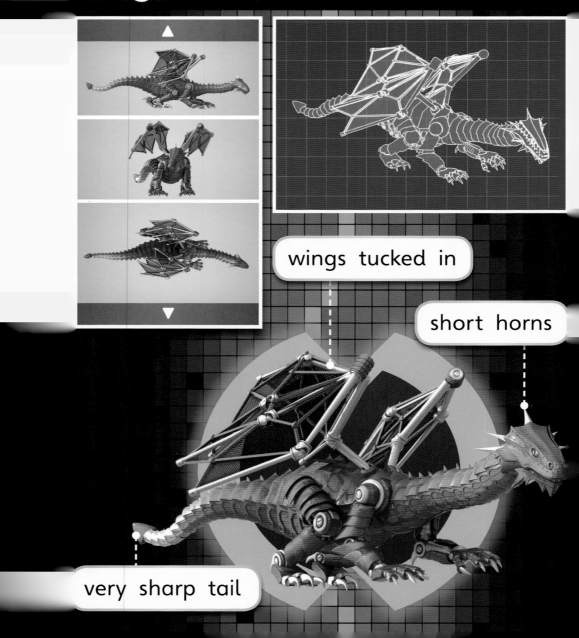

wings tucked in

short horns

very sharp tail

Attack!

Speed | Strength | Combat | Fright

It gets very angry.

bright red

tail will lash

very hot

Stop the BITE!

You need the CODE key to stop the Dragon-BITE and unlock the exit. The CODE key is not on the Dragon-BITE's body.

Mini said, "The CODE key
is not on the BITE's body
so it might be near it.
We have to find the BITE."

"We need the CODE key so we can get to my dad," said Mini.

Now you have read ...
The Dragon-BITE

Text checker

Look on page 7.
What is on the Gizmo screen?

	Yes	No
• A picture with labels.	Yes	No
• A description of what happens next in the story.	Yes	No
• Facts about the BITE.	Yes	No
• A record of what people say in the story.	Yes	No

MITE fun

Can you remember what happened to Mini's dad?

You will never find the CODE key!

11

Before you read

Sound checker
Say the sound.

y

Sound spotter
Blend the sounds.

| l | u | ck | y |

| r | o | ck | y |

| qu | i | ck | l | y |

| y | e | ll | ed |

Tricky words
were
there
have
so

Into the zone

Do you remember what
Max can do with his watch?

The Angry BITE

Max, Ant and Mini were looking
for the CODE key.
The path was very rocky.

"What's that?" asked Ant.
"It could be the Dragon-BITE,"
said Mini.

Suddenly, the BITE swooped down.
"It's there!" yelled Max.

The BITE was angry.
Its claws were big and sharp.
It shot out fire.

We have to run!

The BITE shot fire at Max, Ant and Mini.

"Run!" yelled Max. "I have my watch so I will fight the BITE."

Ant and Mini quickly ran back to the jeep.
"Max is still fighting!" said Mini.

At the last moment, Max jumped
into the jeep.
"Go quickly! The Dragon-BITE
is still there!" he said.

The BITE shot fire at the jeep.
"Quick, Max!" said Ant. "Fight it!"
Max held up his watch.

The BITE fell and hurt its wing. "We were lucky, but we still have to get the CODE key," said Mini.

Now you have read ...
The Angry BITE

Text checker
How did Max protect Ant and Mini from the Dragon-BITE?

MITE fun
Look back at the story. Imagine you are in the jeep with Max, Ant and Mini. What can you hear, see, smell and touch? How do you feel?